José Dario Gallegos

Merchant of the Santa Fe Trail

For the students at Skyview
Elementary.

Con amor,

Emerita Romero-Anderson

José Dario Gallegos
Merchant of the Santa Fe Trail

A NOW YOU  KNOW BIO

Emerita Romero-Anderson

Filter Press, LLC
Palmer Lake, Colorado

For Dario's descendants whose reverence keeps his memory alive.

For my father, George G. Romero, whose foresight keeps Dario's legacy alive.

Library of Congress Control Number: 2007928454
ISBN: 978-0-86541-084-8

Filter Press, LLC, P.O. Box 95, Palmer Lake, Colorado.

Printed in the United States of America

Contents

José Dario Gallegos 1830-1883

Spanish colonial soldiers sailed across the Atlantic Ocean in the sixteenth century to claim the New World for God and for the King of Spain. These conquistadors traveled over the desert of Mexico and into the southern Rocky Mountains.

José Dario Gallegos was a descendant of these *conquistadores.* And in the spirit of the explorers, Dario left New Mexico, Mexico's northernmost frontier, for present-day southern Colorado in 1851 to conquer the land his ancestors had claimed for Spain — not with weapons, but with merchandise and a business plan.

The location for this new venture presented some problems, however. In 1848, Mexico had surrendered the Territory of New Mexico to the United States in the Treaty of Guadalupe Hidalgo. The territory included an unsettled area sixty-five miles north of Taos. This isolated high alpine valley, bordered by the Sangre de Cristo mountain range to the east and the

San Juan mountains to the west, had many natural resources but a very cold climate and Native Americans ready to fight for their hunting grounds.

Dario knew that earlier attempts to settle the valley had been unsuccessful, but he was determined and pushed forward. As a merchant, his goal was to assist his people in establishing a settlement by providing supplies. It would take courage, and he would have to build a store from the ground up. How would he get the supplies needed to stock his store? Would there be enough customers to keep the store going? Dario felt confident he could make it work. He knew he would have to work hard, and because of the distance from trade centers, isolation would be his greatest challenge.

He had learned the trade business early on from his father. Dario had the know-how, and he had the money. But with the uncertainty of the new American government and very little currency flowing in the New Mexico Territory, would Dario be able to fulfill his dream of having his own store that would *sustain* a settlement?

1 A Merchant's Son

José Dario Gallegos was born in Ojo Caliente de Abiquiu, New Mexico, a territory of the Mexican Republic, on December 19, 1830, eighteen years before the Mexican-American War. Ojo Caliente, which literally means "hot spring", is a village with warm, natural springs sixty-five miles west of Taos, New Mexico. His parents, Don José Gabriel Gallegos and Doña Maria Simona del Carmen Baca, had him baptized José Desiderio Gallegos in Taos on December 28 and shortened his name to Dario.

Dario was five when the family moved to Arroyo Seco, a few miles north of Taos. He lived there with his parents until he was nineteen. Dario was the second of nine children. After his mother died, his widowed father remarried twice.

The Gallegos family considered themselves Españoles-Mexicanos, or persons of Spanish ancestry born in Mexico. The surname Gallegos originated in Galicia, a province or region on the northwestern corner of Spain in the Iberian Peninsula. A *Gallego* is a person from Galicia who carried the surname to the New World. The Gallegos surname is believed also to mean, "one who strutted like a rooster."

Christopher Columbus' flagship, the ship flying his flag on the voyage to the New World, was originally named *Gallego*. The ship had been seized in the name of the crown by a friend of Columbus from Juan de la Costa. Although Columbus feared the ship was too deep to clear sandbars and reefs, he had no other ship and changed the name to *Santa Maria* before setting sail in 1492. One of the members of Columbus's crew was named Rodrigo Gallegos.

Another Gallego, Basco, sailed with explorer Ferdinand Magelllan. Magellan commanded the first fleet to circumnavigate the globe, that is to sail completely around the world. In the service of Spain Magellan set sail on September 20, 1519, and died during his voyage of discovery in the Philippines on April 20, 1521.

The Gallegos family coat of arms uses five colors: red, standing for nobility in heart and mind; silver and white, for harmony and sincerity; gold, for generosity; and black, for faithfulness and grief.

As do many families, the Gallegos family has a coat of arms, which is an emblem on a shield with objects or pictures that represent the family. The practice of designing, displaying, describing, and recording coats of arms is nearly nine hundred years old and is called "heraldry" because a herald was a person who made important announcements. Coats of arms were used first to identify a person in battle and later to imprint on a seal of wax, as carvings on a family tomb, and as banners on country homes.

Dario's ancestors came to New Spain (Mexico) from Spain, in the 1500s. The Gallegos family migrated north with conquistadors and missionaries to settle the land and convert American Indians to Christianity. Dario's ancestors were known to be in New Mexico before the Pueblo Revolt of 1680, when the Pueblo Indians drove the Spaniards out of Pueblo lands.

Dario's father, Don José Gabriel, and his uncle, Antonio, operated way stations, which were stopping-places on the Santa Fe Trail for travelers to rest. Trade on the route that became known as the Santa Fe Trail had begun in 1821 when Captain William Becknell set out from Missouri to trade with Indians. He met several New Mexicans along the way who persuaded him to follow them to Santa Fe. The trip was very profitable, and the following year Becknell went again to Santa Fe, traveling this time with a wagon train rather than pack animals. Also in 1821, Mexico, known until then as New Spain, had won its independence from Spain. The Republic of Mexico opened its borders and welcomed trade with the United States. Much of the trade was along the Camino Real, or "royal road," from Santa Fe to Chihuahua, Durango, Lagos, and other markets in Mexico. Now American and New Mexican traders could travel freely to and from Santa Fe and eastern trading centers in St. Louis and Independence, Missouri.

José Gabriel prospered and bought farmland. He grew crops on his farms and sold produce from his way stations to merchants traveling the Santa Fe Trail. Eventually, José Gabriel became a traveling merchant himself, and Dario began learning the trade business from him. As a young boy, Dario looked forward to the day he would be old enough to go with his father on trading trips. He had often heard how the merchants battled heat and thirst, hostile Indians, and bandits along the Santa Fe Trail and the Camino Real.

In spite of all the hardships and dangers, Dario longed to go.

On September 6, 1844, at age thirteen, Dario got his wish. For protection, he and his father traveled in

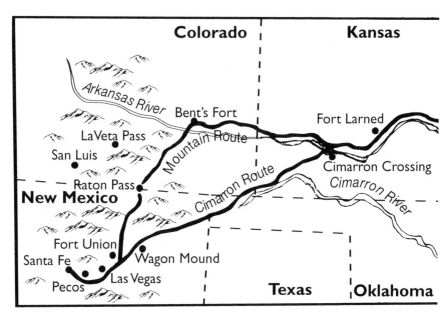

The Santa Fe Trail connected Santa Fe, New Mexico, with major trading centers in Independence and St. Louis, Missouri.

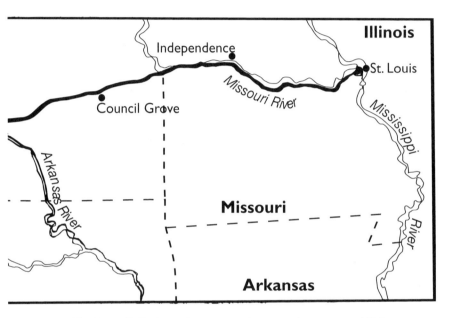

The Santa Fe Trail was the main trading route beginning in 1821 until it was replaced by railroads in 1879.

a caravan of twenty-three merchants. It took 113 days for the caravan of mules and men to reach Chihuahua, Mexico. Dario and his father traded four bundles of domestic merchandise, household goods valued at 100 *pesos*, 6 *reales*, which was a large sum of money. The goods the New Mexicans carried to Chihuahua were crude, locally made products and produce, such as raw wool, buffalo and deer hides, *colchas* (quilts), homemade *serapes*, pine nuts, salt, and Indian blankets. In exchange, they received expensive manufactured goods such as iron tools and weapons, imported fabrics, boots, shoes, chocolate, sugar, ink, and paper to sell in New Mexico.

The journey was a success, and Dario was on his way to becoming a merchant.

2 Pioneer, Settler, Founder

Dario had learned much about the trade business, and like his father, he had a disposition that helped him to succeed as a merchant. He enjoyed talking to people and was comfortable with them. Helping José Gabriel prepare for trading trips taught Dario what he needed to know. He learned how to secure and balance merchandise on the mules. He learned how to obtain a *guía* at the Customs House in Santa Fe. A guía was a document similar to a passport that told who the trader was and when, where, and what was being traded. Dario learned how to estimate the length of a day's trip and to know when to stop to feed the animals. He became an expert in taking care of the mules and other animals, and occasionally acted as a veterinarian and blacksmith.

When Dario was old enough for elementary school, there was little money to pay and keep teachers or build schools in New Mexico. Children learned to read, write, and work with numbers from a *scribe* or a priest. Dario may have attended elementary school in Taos. Taos was one of six towns in New Mexico that by 1831 employed a primary school teacher. When he was older, he may have traveled on the Santa Fe Trail to attend school in *Los Estados Unidos*, the United States.

Until Dario was married at the age of twenty, he lived with his parents in Arroyo Seco. In 1850, Dario married Maria Eulogia Valdez in Taos. Five years later, Dario and his wife started their family.

The westward push of the United States into New Mexican territory was the start of two decades of furious fighting between the U. S. military and American Indian tribes. New Mexicans fought in U.S. territorial *militias* against the Indian tribes and on the side of the United States in the American Civil War. Navajo resistance was finally crushed by the U.S. in 1864.

In those days, it was common for wealthy New Mexican families to buy, trade, or be awarded Indians captured in battle. The number of Indian captives in New Mexican households rose dramatically during the years of conflict between the United States and Native

Americans. By 1868, eight thousand Navajos lived in captivity. In addition to their own nine children, Dario and Eulogia adopted three Navajo children who had come into the family as captive slaves.

Dario and Eulogia's home was next door to his parents' house. Dario continued to farm, travel, and trade with his father. By the age of twenty-seven, he had made enough money to venture out on his own. He owned land in Arroyo Seco worth $900 and owned $1,300 worth of personal property. He was wealthy. He had enough money to open a store on the largest *land grant* ever awarded by the Mexican government, called the Sangre de Cristo Grant. The land grant, which had originally been awarded in 1843, became a United States territory in 1848 after the Mexican-American War. The United States acquired the land grant with the Treaty of Guadalupe Hidalgo and continued its settlement under the terms set by the Mexican government before the war.

The first attempt to settle the Sangre de Cristo Grant on the Rio Culebra, now known as the Culebra River, was *thwarted* by the Ute Indians who had used the valley as their hunting grounds for centuries. The small group of settlers was driven back to the homes they had left behind.

In 1851, a second group of families attempted to establish a settlement along the Rio Culebra in spite of the danger of an attack by the Utes. Dario went with this second group in hopes of establishing a store. The group traveled north sixty-five miles on the wagon road which came to be known as the Taos Trail. It led them to the site of the first settlement. They called their new home San Luis de la Culebra. Because of the dangers, Dario's wife, Eulogia, remained behind in Arroyo Seco. For the settlers' protection, the American War Department built Fort Massachusetts at the base of Sierra Blanca, or Mount Blanca, in 1852. Because the fort was twenty-two miles away, the settlers were still vulnerable to attack.

The head of each of the ninety-five families was given a plot of land measured in *varas* (one *vara* is approximately three feet) by Carlos Beaubien who inherited his son Nariciso's interest in the Sangre de Cristo Grant. Carlos already owned a land grant called the Maxwell Grant, but he wanted to own land in the valley to the north. He had Narcisco, who was twelve at the time, and Stephen Lee, who worked for him, petition the government for the Sangre de Cristo Grant. The grant had been awarded to them by New Mexico Governor Manuel Armijo in 1843. Tragically, Narcisco and Stephen Lee were killed during the Taos Rebellion, an uprising against American occupation of New Mexico, in 1847. According to the terms of the land grant, Carlos had to find people to settle it within two years.

To oversee construction of his store in San Luis de la Culebra, Dario traveled back and forth between the settlement and Arroyo Seco. He hired men to bring large rocks from the *mesa* and mix *adobe* mortar to hold them together for the foundation. The walls were constructed with handmade adobe bricks measuring twenty-four by twelve by four inches. The men spent months cutting huge logs and hand-sawing lumber for

Dario's original store, photographed in 1876.

the roof. The women hand-plastered the outer walls with mud and straw and whitewashed the interior with *tierra blanca*, white dirt brought from mines near Taos. The finished store measured twenty feet wide by forty feet long.

On June 22, 1857, six years after he first came to San Luis, Dario opened the first *mercantile* store in San Luis de la Culebra. This was four years before Colorado became a territory in 1861 and nineteen years before it was admitted to statehood.

On opening day, a small crowd of people gathered in front of the newly completed adobe building to listen to Dario, a handsome man of twenty-seven.

Has not the United States built a fort for the sole purpose of protecting us and our property? It is true that our people are few, but it will not be long before others follow our footsteps to this beautiful valley. I shall place my faith in God.

Dario had invested $452 in *merchandise*. The shelves were stocked with unroasted coffee, salt, dried peas, lentils and beans, white and blue flour, tobacco, a few lengths of calico and gingham cloth, and matches, a fairly new invention at that time. To satisfy the sweet tooth, he offered sun-dried apples and peaches called *orejones*, chocolate imported from Mexico, and *piloncillo*, a cone-shaped cake of unrefined brown sugar that children licked like lollipops.

Dario had his store, but it would be three years before his family joined him in his new home.

Know More!

Copy the list of store items and their prices in the 1850s. Look at store ads online or visit local stores to price the same items at today's cost. Make a graph to show the differences in prices. Show the total amount for the items bought in the 1850s and the total amount for the items bought today.

Cost of items in the 1850s
bar of soap – 15¢
bottle of pain medicine – 40¢
10 lbs. bacon – $3.00
1 pair of leather boots – $6.00

How many choices did the settlers have for each item listed above? Explain.

How many choices and prices can be found for each item in stores today? For example, what was the most expensive brand of soap? Least expensive?

3 Growing a Business

Dario lived in a time of uncertainty and danger. The conquest of New Mexico by armed forces of the United States had begun in 1846 as part of the Americans' drive to expand their territory, which had started with the Louisiana Purchase in 1803. The boundaries of the Louisiana Purchase had bordered Spanish territory until 1821 when it became Mexican territory. Both countries had been on constant alert against American intrusion, but nothing could keep the Americans out.

General Stephen Kearney led his Army of the West down the Santa Fe Trail to Santa Fe, and New Mexico was handed over to the U.S. military forces without firing a shot.

This led to the Taos Rebellion. New Mexicans from the outer communities, including Arroyo Seco where

Dario lived, and Pueblo Indians, came to the defense of Taos. It was the bloodiest act of *rebellion* and the last show of force by Mexicans in the war with the United States.

The Mexican-American War ended in 1848 when the United States and the Mexican governments signed the Treaty of Guadalupe Hidalgo. As a result of the treaty, New Mexico became a territory of the United States in 1850. New Mexico included what is now Colorado. Colorado became a separate U.S. territory in 1861.

After the war, trade along the Santa Fe Trail boomed. However, New Mexicans were met with distrust by the Americans who did not understand Mexican *culture*.

Americans were slow to adjust to the New Mexican traditional methods of trade, which involved very little money. Charles Bent, territorial governor of New Mexico and one of the most famous Americans to settle in the territory, described New Mexicans this way: "These people are *corrupt*, lazy and ignorant. Their character is made up of stupidity and vanity. They are not to be trusted and should be ruled by others than themselves." Bent was one of the Americans killed during the Taos Rebellion.

To the Americans, Dario was a foreigner. It was difficult for him to get loans from American banks. He found a way to solve the problem. Merchants often built their stores close to forts. The location of Fort Massachusetts had become a problem. The Utes could fire their weapons down from the foothills into the fort. In 1858, one year after Dario's store was built, Fort Massachusetts was replaced by Fort Garland. The new fort was six miles closer to the settlement, which gave greater protection to the settlers. And the fort itself gave Dario another group with which to trade.

Selling local farm produce to supply Fort Garland gave Dario American *currency*. This money made it possible for him to establish credit with U.S. banks. He was able to purchase merchandise from American markets, which included European goods, to supply the settlement and the fort.

Dario also traded with the Ute Indians who lived in the area. The Utes enjoyed bartering and liked trading with the settlers when they weren't fighting with them. However, under the new American government, it became illegal to trade with the Utes. And, in 1868, Dario and the settlers witnessed the removal of the Colorado Utes from the valley to reservations in western Colorado.

*Fort Garland about 1890 with Sierra Blanca in the
background. Fort Garland replaced Fort Massachusetts in 1858 to
provide greater protection to the settlers of San Luis.*

With the increasing demand to supply goods to
Fort Garland and to stock his own store, Dario began
his career as a traveling merchant of the Santa Fe Trail.

The trail spanned 970 miles of mountains and
plains between the San Luis Valley and Missouri. His
wagons traveled the San Luis Valley branch of the trail,
going up over La Veta Pass in southern Colorado and
dropping down into Tinaja Canyon in eastern
Huerfano County. Tinaja Canyon had fresh water and
was an excellent place to camp during bad weather.

From there, the wagons headed north to the Arkansas River, which they followed east to Bent's Old Fort, near what is now the town of La Junta, Colorado. After resting and trading for supplies, the wagons moved through Kansas into Missouri and on to St. Louis.

Encouraged by his first year of success in business, Dario equipped a four-wagon mule train in the spring of 1858. He became a common sight as he traveled the trail to St. Louis to buy goods. By then, there were as many as 1,800 wagons traveling the dusty route each year. The nearly 2,000-mile round trip took about six months.

Know More!

Using a map of the San Luis Valley branch of the Santa Fe Trail, follow the path Dario traveled from San Luis de la Culebra to St. Louis, Missouri. Start in San Luis and go northeast over La Veta Pass, then head north to the Arkansas River and follow the river east to Bent's Old Fort. Now go past Kansas and into Missouri and find St. Louis.

On a map of the United States, follow the same route. What present-day highway follows the old Santa Fe Trail? Name one town in each state the trail passes through.

The following year, he outfitted an even larger mule train with six wagons and drivers and set off to fill another order of goods. Those goods included boots and shoes, as well as knives, fabric, silk thread, hats, and silk gloves. On the return trip, as the caravan approached a point near La Junta, in present-day Colorado, it was overtaken by a band of Plains Indians who stole the merchandise and draft animals. The wagons were set on fire. Luckily, Dario and his drivers escaped on horseback into a thicket above the Arkansas River and escaped with their lives.

In spite of the setback, Dario continued to risk the dangers to keep his store stocked with American and European goods from the East, as well as merchandise from the Santa Fe trade to the south. His hard work was rewarded by a period of good fortune. His success allowed him to extend credit to his customers and barter for goods and labor.

Dario thrived as a merchant and helped sustain San Luis de la Culebra and other new settlements that sprang up in the San Luis Valley.

4 A Man of Vision

Dario's vision, courage, and faith in God led him to success and a position of prominence. He had earned the right to add "Don" in front of his name when he achieved the status of Hidalgo de Solar Conocido. This is a social status below petty nobility and given to well-bred persons of good family standing. The communities grew, and with growth came other challenges and needs. Dario's contributions to the success of the settlements went beyond establishing the first mercantile business in the San Luis Valley.

Because the valley received little rainfall, *acequias*, an irrigation system to water crops, were needed. The acequias carried the water from the Culebra River to the fields. Don Dario and everyone who needed water dug the San Luis People's Ditch and established the first water rights in Colorado on April 10, 1852. This gave the settlers the rights to water flowing off the Sangre de Cristo watershed into the Culebra River, which cut through the south edge of the settlement.

Don Dario owned a vast amount of property and farmland. Costilla County, Colorado, records show that in 1865, he bought 100 *varas* of land from Buenaventura Lucero "lying within the county of Costilla in the Territory of Colorado." The records also show that in 1872, he bought buildings, corrals, and barns from Amador Sanchez. The same source records that twelve original settlers transferred title of their properties to Salazar and Gallegos. Arcadio

Know More!

Acequias are ditches that carry water to crops. Water from snow melt and rain flows off the mountains and into rivers. Ditches, or acequias, dug from the river carry water to the fields. This irrigation system has been in use in San Luis de la Culebra since 1852.

Why is it necessary to divert water? What is a semi-arid climate? Name crops grown in the San Luis Valley in Dario's lifetime. Are the same crops grown there today?

The San Luis People's Ditch gave what are known as *priority one water rights* to Dario and the settlers of San Luis de la Culebra. Explain what those water rights were.

ORIGINAL WATER RIGHTS
DECREED TO

DARIO GALLEGOS   SOLEDAD PACHECO
DONACIANO GALLEGOS   FRANCISCO BARELA
JUAN A. TRUJILLO   ISABEL PACHECO
MARIA ROSA VIGIL   ROBERTO ALLEN
JOSE YLARIO VALDEZ   MARIANO PACHECO
E. JARAMILLO   JUAN PACHECO
EULALDA GALLEGOS   JUAN ANTONIO
EULOGIA GALLEGOS   L. A. SALAZAR
RAFAELA SANCHEZ   EULOGIA
JUAN MARTINEZ   JUAN
FRANCISCO VALDEZ   ANTONIO
MANUEL VIGIL
EUSEBIO VARGAS
JUAN VALDEZ
FRANCISCO

Plaque commemorating the San Luis People's Ditch, the oldest continuously used irrigation ditch in Colorado, and the grant of original water rights on April 10, 1852. The plaque reads, "Colorado's greatness is built upon irrigation. Erected by the State Historical Society of Colorado, the heirs of the pioneers, and the Irrigation Centennial Commission, April 10, 1952."

Salazar became a partner in 1874. After the death of Don Dario's widow in 1912, three of his grandsons formed a company called The Gallegos Brothers and bought a few hundred acres of the ancestral farmland from Dario's heirs. Today, three of Don Dario's great-great-grandsons and one great-great-great-grandson farm these centennial farms. A centennial farm is a farm kept in the same family for at least one hundred years.

Don Dario built a small chapel about 200 yards east of where the Sangre de Cristo Parish Church stands in the town of San Luis today. Don Dario and Eulogia dedicated it to Saint Joseph. Because religious life was at the very heart of the community, and

Irrigation ditches, or acequias, have brought water to farms in the San Luis Valley since 1852.

because mission priests came through only occasionally, the chapel helped meet the spiritual needs of the settlers. The Penitentes, a four-centuries-old religious brotherhood, also helped maintain the functions of the church. These men lived in the settlement and provided community service, such as helping to care for those in need.

Ceran St. Vrain built the first mill for grinding grain into flour. He opened the American Flour Company in San Luis de la Culebra in 1859 with his business partner, Harvey Easterday. The settlers no longer had to take their grain to Taos to be ground into flour, and Don Dario was able to buy flour from the flour company to sell in his store.

In 1874, Arcadio Salazar married Don Dario's second-oldest daughter, Genoveva, and became a partner in the store. The union of the two families and the coming of the railroads, brought many changes to the business. In 1879, use of the Santa Fe Trail as a trading route came to an end.

At the time, railroads were being built across the United States making it easier to transport goods. Don Dario and his new partner, who was also his son-in-law, now had a faster and better way of bringing more goods to the settlements. The Atchison, Topeka &

Santa Fe Railroad was built on a path parallel to the Santa Fe Trail. Goods were shipped by rail to the end-of-the-line town and then transported in wagons along the rest of the trail.

In 1881, the D&RG (Denver and Rio Grande) laid track from the north down the Rio Grande River, from Fort Garland to Española, which is 18 miles north of Santa Fe, New Mexico. The Chili Line, as it was called, carried farm produce from Antonito, Colorado, to Española and brought from New Mexico chilis, and many vegetables and fruits. The train also brought construction supplies to enlarge Dario's store to 120 feet in length and build a new shingled roof.

As farming grew, Don Dario and Arcadio brought the first John Deere steel plow to Colorado, as well as the first threshing machine, which was used to separate the seeds from the grain-bearing plant and was powered by two horses mounted on a treadmill. They are also credited with buying the state's first mowing machine, binder and rake, and for planting the first alfalfa field protected by a barbed wire fence.

Don Dario's dream of serving his people had come true.

5 Life of a Merchant

As the aristocratic Spaniards had done when settling Mexico, Don Dario brought his family to their new home after everything was settled and safe. Sometime after 1860, his wife, Eulogia, and the four oldest children came to live in the settlement. Don Dario's house stands today next to his store, in the town of San Luis, Colorado. It is a colonial adobe structure with a southern colonial look, and has been nominated for inclusion in the National Register of Historic Places. The name San Luis de la Culebra was shortened in 1860 when Harvey Easterday petitioned the U.S. Post Master General for grant of a post office to be called San Luis.

San Luis was built as a plaza with a number of flat-roofed adobe houses joined together to form a rectangle. Two large wooden gates closed off the

Dario's house as it looks today on Main Street in San Luis, Colorado.

openings on the two ends to corral the animals at night and protect the settlers.

Don Dario and the settlers were law-abiding, God-fearing people who wanted the best for their families. The residents of San Luis published a town ordinance, or law, and posted a set of town rules dated May 1863. The ordinance spelled out the settlers' rights for the use of pasture, firewood, water, and timber. The ordinance stated:

> All who come as settlers shall agree to abide by the rules and regulations…and be provided with necessary weapons for the defense of the settlement.

The settlers of San Luis agreed to these rules:

1. To maintain the cleanliness of the town and not consent that there be placed therein any nuisance.

2. That drunken revels will not be permitted in the presence of families of the town, nor fights nor similar disorders.

3. That no person from outside will be admitted to live in the town, without having previously presented himself before the Judge or Justice of the Peace and received his permission.

4. It is not permitted that any obstruction be placed in the entrances and outlets of the town.

5. Every one who wishes to take a dwelling or lots in the town, will have to request it of the Judge, paying its value which will remain for the benefit of the chapel.

Don Dario knew the importance of education. The first schools in the settlement were private or operated by the Catholic Church. In 1856, District #1 had been established in San Luis de la Culebra. It was said that Dario sent Guadalupe, his adopted Navajo daughter to Santa Fe, to refine her Spanish and to learn to read and write. As an adult, she helped run the household and became tutor to the younger children in Dario's household. His Navajo son was trained as a horse breeder for the stables.

Because the settlers were dependent on their livestock, Don Dario sometimes went to El Paso, Texas, to buy cattle and sheep. While he was away, Eulogia did the buying and selling for the store, and Don Dario's uncle, José Nasario, helped her run it.

Trail travelers experienced many hardships — dust storms, muddy conditions, insect bites, extremely hot or cold temperatures, hailstorms, strong winds, blizzards, and prairie fires. Come rain or shine, Don Dario rose at dawn with the others to round up and hitch the animals and hit the trail. Stopping midmorning, they unhitched and grazed the teams, hauled water, and gathered wood or buffalo chips for fuel. Then the day's main meal was cooked. After the meal, they repaired wagons, yokes, and harnesses, and greased wagon wheels. If animals were sick, Don Dario helped doctor them. In the afternoon, they moved on, crossing streams that sometimes swelled from rain. At day's end, necessary repairs were made again. Then Don Dario assigned night guards to protect them from the dangers of trail travel. When possible, he enjoyed a few hours of well-earned sleep.

Don Dario was probably on one of his trail trips when he became ill. On January 26, 1883, he passed away at the age of 53. He is buried in the Old San Luis Cemetery in the foothills of the majestic Sangre de Cristo ("Blood of Christ") mountain range. His tombstone reads, "*Amado esposo de Maria Eulogia Valdez de Gallegos. En memoria, RIP.*"

Don José Dario Gallegos accomplished what he'd dreamed of, even though he died at such a young age. During his lifetime, the San Luis de la Culebra settlement grew into a community of about 1,000 people, sharing a common culture and heritage. His store became the favorite meeting place, where people gathered around the potbellied stove to chat and catch up on the latest news and local gossip.

In 1957, for the store's centennial, or 100 year, celebration, the San Luis community came together to honor the oldest mercantile establishment in Colorado and to pay tribute to its founder, Don Dario Gallegos.

Dario's tombstone reads in translation, "Beloved husband of
Maria Eulogia Valdez de Gallegos. In memory, RIP."

COSTUMES DEPICT BY-GONE ERA
In costume around an old Metz automobile are Katherine Gallegos, Alice Smith, Karen Smith, Elena Gallegos, Louise Smith, Patsy Carpenter and Kathleen Gallegos.

19 YEARS BEFORE STATEHOOD

Oldest Colorado Store Marks Centennial

By FRED R. BAKER
Denver Post Staff Writer

SAN LUIS, Colo., June 25.— A crowd of 500 persons gathered in San Luis over the weekend to pay homage to the first and oldest mercantile establishment of Colorado.

The centennial of the Salazar store of San Luis, established in 1857, was marked by historical displays, street dancing, an outline of the history of the area and the store, a picnic lunch at the Val Verde ranch games and races.

Host for the occasion was Delfino Salazar, present head of the Salazar store and owner of the Don Carlos Hotel.

Salazar's interests are not confined to the store and hotel, however, as he owns more than 12,000 acres of land and has more than 90,000 acres under lease for farming and livestock operations.

The store was opened in 1857 by Dario Gallegos, 19 years before Colorado was admitted to statehood. In 1874 A. A. Salazar, father of Delfino, went into partnership with Gallegos.

A history of the early days of the mercantile business was given by Mrs. Belinda Salazar Carpenter, attired in dress dating back to 1895. Mrs. Carpenter spoke from the balcony of the Don Carlos Hotel and the spectators crowded main street to hear her.

In the lobby of the Don Carlos, and in the Salazar store next door, were displays of articles dating back to the founding of the mercantile business.

Display windows of the store were decorated in old-time theme and matrons and young ladies of San Luis donned costumes of the 1880's to be living models in the windows.

After ceremonies in San Luis the crowd traveled to the Val Verde ranch for a picnic lunch.

A baseball game between youngsters and oldsters, was one feature of the afternoon program, which included other group games and races.

State Beet Output

Colorado led Rocky Mountain states in production of sugar beets last year, the U. S. department of agriculture reported. The state supplied 1,893,000 tons of beets which were grown on 120,700 acres. Average yield was 15.7 tons per acre. Cash payments to Colorado growers on the 1956 crop to date are estimated to be more than $26 million.

DELFINO SALAZAR
Marks centennial.

The community of San Luis celebrated the 100th birthday of Don Dario's store with a weekend of festivities. His descendants wore costumes from the 1880s. There were historical displays, music, and street dancing. After ceremonies in San Luis, more than five hundred guests traveled with their host, Delfinio Salazar, Dario's grandson, to the Val Verde Ranch for a picnic. Originally printed in the Denver Post.

SAN LUIS STORE MARKS 100TH BIRTHDAY
Square dancing in the street in front of the Salazar store and Don Carlos hotel in San Luis, Colo., featured the store's 100th birthday Saturday. Store is state's oldest.

From a Denver Post *article of June 25, 1957.*

Three great-great-grandchildren of Dario Gallegos, first owner of the Salazar store model costumes. Shown are Elena and Marie Gallegos and Patsy Carpenter.

Music at the picnic following birthday observance at the Salazar store was furnished by this trio. Shown are (from left) Frank Garcia, Epie Valdez and Sam Bernal.

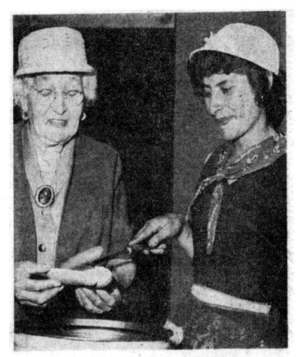

PLENTY OF FOOD FOR CELEBRATION
Mrs. Delfino Salazar, left, wife of the store owner, gets a picnic hot dog from Oliva Vigil. 500 persons attended.

6 A Lasting Legacy

Don Dario's store still operates today, despite having been destroyed twice by fire. In 1895, the first fire left only the adobe walls standing. Dario's son-in-law, Arcadio Salazar, the owner at the time of the first fire, resumed business within three days. He began to rebuild on what was left of the walls within thirty days. In 1947, another fire burned the store almost to the ground, but the old pioneer spirit came through again. This time, the store was rebuilt by Delfino, Arcadio's son. Within a week, it was business as usual.

Today, the two-story building has a grocery and hardware store. Visitors can see some of the original adobe walls in the Spanish-style structure. It is owned and operated by Don Dario's great-granddaughter, Joyce Gallegos-Romero, his great-great-grandson, Felix G. Romero, and his wife, Claudia.

Dario's store in 1929 when it was owned by Delfino Salazar.

In July 2001, the San Luis community celebrated the 150th anniversary of San Luis. June 2007 marked the 150th anniversary of the store. In some ways, little has changed from the way Don Dario ran the business and how R&R Market is operated today. Supplies still come from great distances; the same building site is still used; great-great-grandson and his wife run the business as did Dario and Eulogia; both great-great-grandfather and great-great-grandson have extended credit and bartered for goods and labor; seventeenth-century Spanish is still spoken along with English to

George G. Romero bought the mercantile business in 1969. At that time, it had been owned by the same family for 112 years. Following George Romero's death in 2001, his wife, Joyce, and their son, Felix, became co-owners.

R&R Market, photographed in 2006, is on the
west side of Main Street in San Luis.

conduct business; some of the same products such as
piloncillo, chicos, and ground blue corn for *atole* are still
stocked; and people still gather to tell stories and gossip.

For Don Dario, his desire to provide a place where
the people of the valley could trade compelled him to
succeed. His ambition and perseverance made it possible for the settlement of San Luis to survive. Today, it
is the oldest town in Colorado, and Dario's store has
remained in the same family for 150 years making it
the oldest continuous business in the state.

Don Dario's legacy lives on in his business.

Timeline

1500 – Dario's ancestors arrive in New Spain, now Mexico

1680 – The Gallegos family name is recorded by Fray Angélico Chavez in *Origins of New Mexico Families*

1803 – Louisiana Purchase

1830 – Dario is born in Ojo Caliente de Abiquiu, New Mexico, a territory of the Mexican Republic

1835 – Dario's family moves to Arroyo Seco, north of Taos, New Mexico

1844 – Dario travels with father to trade in Chihuahua, Mexico

1846 – Conquest of New Mexico by the United States

1847 – Taos Rebellion

1850 – Dario marries Maria Eulogia Valdez

1851 – Settlement of San Luis de la Culebra founded on the Sangre de Cristo land grant

1852 – Dario helps build San Luis People's Ditch

Fort Massachusetts is built

1857 – Dario opens first business in San Luis de la Culebra

1858 – Fort Garland is built to replace Fort Massachusetts

1860 – Dario's wife and four children move to San Luis de la Culebra

1874 – Arcadio Salazar marries Dario's daughter, Genoveva

1879 – The Santa Fe Trail closes

1881 – Track is laid for a train between Fort Garland and Española

1883 – Don Dario Gallegos dies at age 53

1895 – Dario's store is destroyed by fire and rebuilt

1947 – Store burns down second time and is rebuilt

1957 – Centennial celebration of Dario's store

2001 – 150th anniversary of the town of San Luis

2007 – 150th anniversary of Dario's store

New Words

adobe – sun-dried bricks made from mud, clay, and straw

ancestry – family tree; bloodline of family descent

atole – cornmeal mush

chicos – dried corn for cooking

conquistadores – sixteenth-century Spanish conquerors of Mexico

corrupt – dishonest

culture – the arts, beliefs, customs, institutions, and all other products created by a people

currency – any form of money in use in a country

descendant – a person considered born from a specified ancestor

land grant – a gift of land given for the purpose or settlement to a group or individual by a government

mercantile – of or related to merchants or trade

merchandise – things that may be bought or sold

mesa – a flat-topped hill or small plateau with steep sides

militias – male military forces that are on call in times of emergency

pesos – monetary unit of Mexico

petty nobility – a social class distinguished by hereditary rank, wealth, power, and privilege

reales – monetary units of Mexico (eight reales equals one peso)

rebellion – an uprising intended to change or overthrow an existing government by means of force

scribe – a writer

serapes – shawls or blankets worn as an outer garment

sustain – to maintain or supply with things needed

thwarted – prevented from taking place

For Further Study

Visit: R&R Market, 367 Main Street, San Luis, Colorado

Visit: San Luis Museum and Cultural Center, 402 Church Place, San Luis, Colorado

Read: Bentley, Nancy, "One Man, One Town, One Culture," *Colorado Fever*, 1, no. 6 (1983): 23 25.

Read: Dutton, Dorothy and Caryl Humphries, *A Rendezvous with Colorado History,* Boise, Ida.: Sterling Ties Publications, (1999), 91 108.

Read: Romero-Anderson, J. Emerita, "Colorado's Oldest Established Business: Two Men-Six Generations," *Celebración San Luis: 150 Years*, Pueblo, Colo.: El Escritorio Publications, 2001, p. 26.

Read: Romero-Anderson, J. Emerita, "My Colorado: Colorado Roots," *Encompass,* May June 2002, 52.

Related Web Sites

http://www.rootsweb.com/~cocostil/history.htm
Brief history of Costillo County, Colorado. The web site states, "Costilla County, Colorado is one of Colorado's original counties, formed in 1861. Prior to 1861 any records will be found in Taos County, New Mexico. The county was named for the Costilla River, which means "little rib" in Spanish. San Luis is the County Seat."

http://www.bicknell.net/sftrail.htm
More about William Becknell, who is called "The Father of the Santa Fe Trail."

http://www.nps.gov/archive/beol/learn_people.htm
Learn more about the brothers Charles and William Bent, owners of Bent's Old Fort on the Santa Fe Trail.

http://www.museumtrail.org/FortMassachusetts.asp
Description of Fort Massachusetts, established in 1852 and replaced by Fort Garland in 1858.

http://extras.denverpost.com/slideshows/latino_slideshow_day4.html
Enjoy photographs from beautiful San Luis valley

http://www.museumtrail.org/SanLuisMuseum.asp
Learn about the San Luis Museum and Cultural Center.

http://www.sanluispreservation.com/
News and photos from San Luis and the Gallegos family

http://www.coloradohistory.org/
A wealth of historical information, photos, and more.

http://www.coloradohistory.org/hist_sites/ft_Garland/ft_garland.htm
For photos and information about Fort Garland Colorado Historic Site.

http://www.hispanicgen.org/
  Colorado Society of Hispanic Genealogy.
  According to the website, "CSHG promotes genealogical and historical research and education to expand the awareness, knowledge, and appreciation of Hispanic culture, history, and traditions."

http://www.laplaza.org/community/about_taos/history/sovereignty.html
  A brief history of Taos, New Mexico. Includes the Taos Rebellion.

http://www.hsnm.org/
  Official web site of the Historical Society of New Mexico

http://www.nmgs.org/
  New Mexico Genealogical Society

Sources

Abstract of Title to San Luis Land, Costilla County, Colorado Survey, Map A, Book E, (1913), 98.

Armstrong, Sperry, *The Voyages of Christopher Columbus.* Chicago: Spenser Press, Landmark Books, 1950, p. 89.

Bean, Luther E. *Land of the Blue Sky People.* Alamosa, Colo.: Ye Olde Print Shoppe, 1975.

Boyle, Susan Calafate. *Los Capitalistas: Hispano Merchants and the Santa Fe Trade.* Albuquerque: University of New Mexico Press, 1997.

Carpenter, Belinda S. "Commemorative Centennial Speech." Office of the Superintendent of Schools, San Luis, Colorado, 1957.

Carson, Phil. *Across the Northern Frontier: Spanish Explorations in Colorado.* Boulder, Colo.: Johnson Books, 1998.

Chavez, Fray Angélico. *Origins of New Mexico Families: In the Spanish Colonial Period.* Santa Fe, N.M.: William Gannon, 1975.

Cheetham, Francis T. *"*The Early Settlements of Southern Colorado.*" The Colorado Magazine* V, no. 1: 6.

Colville, Ruth Marie. *Mt. Lookout "Where you can see for two days. . .,"* Del Norte, Colo.: Benson Enterprises, 1996.

de Onís, José. *The Hispanic Contribution to the State of Colorado.* Boulder: Westview Press, 1976.

Echevarría, Evelio and José Otero. *Hispanic Colorado.* Fort Collins: Centennial Publications, 1976.

Foster, David. "Salazar and Gallegos." *Rocky Mountain Food Dealer.* Denver: August, 1972, pp. 4-6.

Gallegos, Eloy J. *Jacona: An Epic Story of the Spanish Southwest.* Knoxville: Villagra Press, 1996.

Gallegos, Esperanza Hope. *Antepasados de Esperanza "Hope" Gallegos.* Arvada: Hope Gallegos, 2004.

Horgan, Paul. *Great River: The Rio Grande in North American History.* Hanover: Wesleyan University Press, 1984.

Martinez, Maria C. "Don Dario and the Gallegos Legacy." *La Sierra,* January 3, 2003, pp. 1, 6, 7.

Poling-Kempes, Leslie. *Valley of Shining Stone: The Story of Abiquiu.* Tucson: The University of Arizona Press, 1997.

Quintana, Frances Leon. *Pobladores: Hispanic Americans of the Ute Frontier.* Notre Dame: University of Notre Dame Press, 1991.

Simmons, Virginia McConnell. *The San Luis Valley: Land of the Six-Armed Cross.* 2d ed. Niwot: University Press of Colorado, 1999.

Southwest Technology Development Institute. "Ojo Caliente: America's Oldest Spa?" *GHC Bulletin.* Las Cruces: New Mexico State University, 2002.

Trujillo, Marie Oralia Duran. *Autumn Memories: My New Mexico Roots and Traditions.* Pueblo: El Escritorio Publications, 1999.

Tushar, Olibama Lopez. *People of El Valle: A History of Spanish Colonials in the San Luis Valley.* Pueblo: El Escritorio Publications, 1992.

Weber, David J. *On the Edge of Empire: The Taos Hacienda of Los Martinez.* Santa Fe: Museum of New Mexico Press, 1996.

Index

About the Author

Children's author J. Emerita Romero-Anderson grew up in San Luis, Colorado, where she lived the life inherited from her Spanish colonial ancestors. She is the author of a picture book entitled *Grandpa's Tarima,* which found a home in The Sunshine Shared Reading program, McGraw-Hill/The Wright Group. Emerita retired from teaching after a career of twenty-seven years to research and write stories for children.

Acknowledgments

This book was written with the help of librarians, family accounts, the helpful staff at the Costilla County Courts, San Luis Museum and Cultural Center, Family History Library in La Jara, Colorado, Pikes Peak Library District-Special Collections (genealogy, local history), Colorado Historical Society, Fort Garland Museum and Library, National Register of Historic Places, Old San Luis Cemetery, Land Abstracts of San Luis, State Historical Library at Santa Fe, Adams State College Library, Colorado College Tutt Library, Fort Burgwin Library in Taos, N.M., *La Sierra* newspaper, Augustine Gallegos, member, Colorado Society of Hispanic Genealogy, and our local genealogist, Maria C. Martinez. Their commitment to assist those of us writing about and sharing the stories of our ancestors is key to the preservation of our way of life for future generations. A sincere thanks to my husband, Kent, for his support and assistance throughout, and to publisher Doris Baker, for allowing me to tell Don Dario's story.

More
Now You Know Bios

Justina Ford:
Medical Pioneer
ISBN: 0-86541-074-7
$8.95
Joyce B. Lohse

Martha Maxwell:
Natural History Pioneer
ISBN: 987-0-86541-075-6
$8.95
James McVey

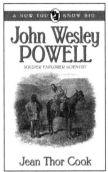

John Wesley Powell:
Soldier Explorer Scientist
ISBN: 978-0-86541-080-0
$8.95
Jean Thor Cook

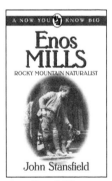

Enos Mills:
Rocky Mountain Naturalist
ISBN: 978-0-86541-072-5
$8.95
John Stansfield

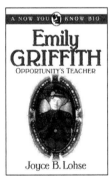

Emily Griffith:
Opportunity's Teacher
ISBN: 987-0-86541-077-0
$8.95
Joyce B. Lohse

Unsinkable:
The Molly Brown Story
ISBN: 978-0-86541-081-7
$8.95
Joyce B. Lohse

Now You Know Bios are available at your local bookstore,
by calling 888.570.2663, and online at
www.filterpressbooks.com